Jump from the Stump

Kelly Doudna

Consulting Editor, Diane Craig, M.A./Reading Specialist

ABDO
Publishing Company

Published by ABDO Publishing Company, 4940 Viking Drive, Edina, Minnesota 55435.

Printed in the United States.

Credits
Edited by: Pam Price
Curriculum Coordinator: Nancy Tuminelly
Cover and Interior Design and Production: Mighty Media
Photo Credits: Photodisc, Rubberball Productions

Library of Congress Cataloging-in-Publication Data

Doudna, Kelly, 1963-
    Jump from the stump / Kelly Doudna.
        p. cm. -- (First rhymes)
    Includes index.
    ISBN 1-59679-485-2 (hardcover)
    ISBN 1-59679-486-0 (paperback)
        1. English language--Rhyme--Juvenile literature. I. Title. II. Series.
PE1517.D6836 2005
808.1--dc22
                                                                    2005048786

SandCastle™ books are created by a professional team of educators, reading specialists, and content developers around five essential components that include phonemic awareness, phonics, vocabulary, text comprehension, and fluency. All books are written, reviewed, and leveled for guided reading and early intervention reading, and designed for use in shared, guided, and independent reading and writing activities to support a balanced approach to literacy instruction.

Let Us Know

After reading the book, SandCastle would like you to tell us your stories about reading. What is your favorite page? Was there something hard that you needed help with? Share the ups and downs of learning to read. We want to hear from you! To get posted on the ABDO Publishing Company Web site, send us e-mail at:

sandcastle@abdopub.com

SandCastle Level: Beginning

-ump

clump

dump

hump

jump

stump

We see a ![handwritten: clump] .

Here is the .

dump

I look at a .

hump

I see him .

We see the stump .

The flowers are
in a clump.

The dump is smelly.

The camel
has a hump.

Ron can jump high.

The stump is brown.

Jump from the Stump

The camel has a hump.

The camel with a hump
is on a stump.

The camel with a hump
is on a stump
next to the dump.

The camel with a hump
on the stump
sees flowers in a clump
behind the dump.

The camel with a hump
must jump
from the stump
to get a good look
at the clump
behind the dump.

About SandCastle™

A professional team of educators, reading specialists, and content developers created the SandCastle™ series to support young readers as they develop reading skills and strategies and increase their general knowledge. The SandCastle™ series has four levels that correspond to early literacy development in young children. The levels are provided to help teachers and parents select the appropriate books for young readers.

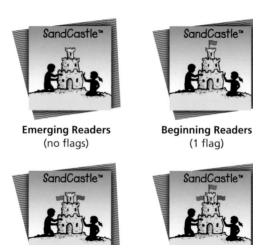

Emerging Readers
(no flags)

Beginning Readers
(1 flag)

Transitional Readers
(2 flags)

Fluent Readers
(3 flags)

These levels are meant only as a guide. All levels are subject to change.

To see a complete list of SandCastle™ books and other nonfiction titles from ABDO Publishing Company, visit www.abdopub.com or contact us at:
4940 Viking Drive, Edina, Minnesota 55435 • 1-800-800-1312 • fax: 1-952-831-1632